CELLS

SUPER COOL SCIENCE EXPERIMENTS: CELLS

by Matt Mullins

CHERRY LAKE PUBLISHING • ANN ARBOR, MICHIGAN

A NOTE TO PARENTS AND TEACHERS: Please review the instructions for these experiments before your children do them. Be sure to help them with any experiments you do not think they can safely conduct on their own.

A NOTE TO KIDS: Be sure to ask an adult for help with these experiments when you need it. Always put your safety first!

Published in the United States of America by
Cherry Lake Publishing
Ann Arbor, Michigan
www.cherrylakepublishing.com

Content Editor: Robert Wolffe, EdD,
Professor of Teacher Education,
Bradley University, Peoria, Illinois

Book design and illustration: The Design Lab

Photo Credits: Cover and page 1, ©Clearviewstock/Dreamstime.com; page 7, ©iStockphoto.com/ArtisticCaptures; page 11, ©Medical-on-Line/Alamy; page 12, ©iStockphoto.com/DOConnell; page 16, ©Jubal Harshaw, used under license from Shutterstock, Inc.; page 20, ©iStockphoto.com/NNehring; page 24, ©Photo Network/Alamy; page 25, ©WaterFrame/Alamy

Library of Congress Cataloging-in-Publication Data
Mullins, Matt.
Super cool science experiments: Cells / by Matt Mullins.
p. cm.—(Science explorer)
Includes bibliographical references and index.
ISBN-13: 978-1-60279-517-4 ISBN-10: 1-60279-517-7 (lib. bdg.)
ISBN-13: 978-1-60279-596-9 ISBN-10: 1-60279-596-7 (pbk.)
1. Cells—Experiments—Juvenile literature. I. Title. II. Title: Cells.
III. Series.
QH582.5.M85 2010
571.6078—dc22 2009004770

Cherry Lake Publishing would like to acknowledge the work of The Partnership for 21st Century Skills. Please visit *www.21stcenturyskills.org* for more information.

CELLS

TABLE OF CONTENTS

We Can All Study Cells!

When you think of science, what comes to mind? Do you picture adults planning important experiments? Science is an amazing tool that helps people learn new things. And guess what? You don't have to wait until you are a grown-up to start thinking like a scientist. You can begin now. If you like to find answers to interesting questions, you are on your way to becoming a scientist!

Believe it or not, you can do experiments with things you already have at home or things that you can easily obtain. In this book, we'll learn how scientists think. We'll do that by experimenting with cells—the tiny structures that make up living things. We'll even discover how to design our own experiments. The best part is we'll find out new information and have fun along the way!

First Things First

Scientists learn by studying something very carefully. For example, scientists who focus on cells watch how they grow and what they do. They use microscopes and other equipment to see how cells make more cells and react to different environments.

Good scientists take notes on everything they discover. They write down their observations. Sometimes those observations lead scientists to ask new questions. With new questions in mind, they design experiments to find the answers.

When scientists plan experiments, they must think very clearly. The way they think about problems is often called the scientific method. What is the scientific method? It's a step-by-step way of finding answers to specific questions. The steps don't always follow the same pattern. Sometimes scientists change their minds. The process often works something like this:

- **Step One:** A scientist gathers the facts and makes observations about one particular thing.
- **Step Two:** The scientist comes up with a question that is not answered by all the observations and facts.
- **Step Three:** The scientist creates a hypothesis. This is a statement of what the scientist thinks is probably the answer to the question.
- **Step Four:** The scientist tests the hypothesis. He or she designs an experiment to see whether the hypothesis is correct. The scientist does the experiment and writes down what happens.
- **Step Five:** The scientist draws a conclusion based on how the experiment turned out. The conclusion might be that the hypothesis is correct. Sometimes, though, the hypothesis is not correct. In that case, the scientist might develop a new hypothesis and another experiment.

In the following experiments, we'll see the scientific method in action. First, we'll gather some facts and observations about cells. For each experiment, we'll also develop a question and a hypothesis. Next, we'll do the experiment to see if our hypothesis is correct. By the end of the experiment, we should know something new about cells. Scientists, are you ready? Then let's get started!

Experiment #1 Cells Are Small

People are multicellular. Each person has trillions of cells!

Cells are the smallest living structures in any living thing, or organism. All organisms have cells. Some living things are multicellular. They might be made of billions of cells. Other organisms are unicellular. This means that they have just a single cell.

Do you want to see what a cell looks like? Scientists have tips and tricks to help them study cells. One important tool that scientists use to look at cells is a microscope. Even using a microscope, however, a cell can sometimes be difficult to see.

Think about your fingerprint. If you look at your thumb, you can probably make out the swirls and lines on your skin. But if you lightly color over your thumbprint with a marker, you might be able to see your print easier. By now, you may be asking yourself the following question: **Can adding dye to a cell make it easier to see its different parts?** Here is one possible hypothesis: **Using dye *will* make it easier to see the different parts of a cell.** Want to see if this hypothesis is right?

Here's what you'll need:

- A knife
- An onion
- A pair of tweezers
- A clean microscope slide
- A water or medicine dropper
- A drop of water
- A clean microscope coverslip
- A microscope
- A drop of iodine

Gather your supplies.

Instructions:

1. Use the knife to cut the onion in half. Ask an adult for help if you need it. Peel away the 2 outside layers and discard them. With your tweezers, carefully remove a section of the thin skin from the outside of a layer of the onion.
2. Lay the small piece of onion on the slide. Then use a medicine dropper to place a drop of water on the onion sample.
3. Place the coverslip over the water and the onion. Try your best to keep air bubbles from forming under the coverslip. Next, gently place the slide under your microscope. Look at the onion cells, adjusting the microscope power and light until you can see them well. What do you notice? Record all your observations, and draw some of the cells you see.

4. Now gently remove your slide from the microscope, and place a drop of iodine on a corner of the coverslip. The iodine should eventually make its way under the coverslip. Set the slide aside for 4 minutes to let the iodine stain the onion cells.
5. Then place the slide under the microscope once more. Remember to adjust the power and light until you can see the cells well. What do you notice about them this time? Write down everything you observe, and draw more pictures.

Conclusion:

Think about your observations and compare the pictures you drew. Was it easier to see the cells with or without the iodine?

In 1665, English scientist Robert Hooke described what he found when he examined a slice of cork with a simple microscope. He saw that it seemed to be made up of many "little boxes." These boxes reminded him of the small rooms, or cells, of a monastery. Hooke therefore concluded that cork, which is made from the wood of a living tree, contained what he called cells.

Experiment #2 Not Huge, but Hungry

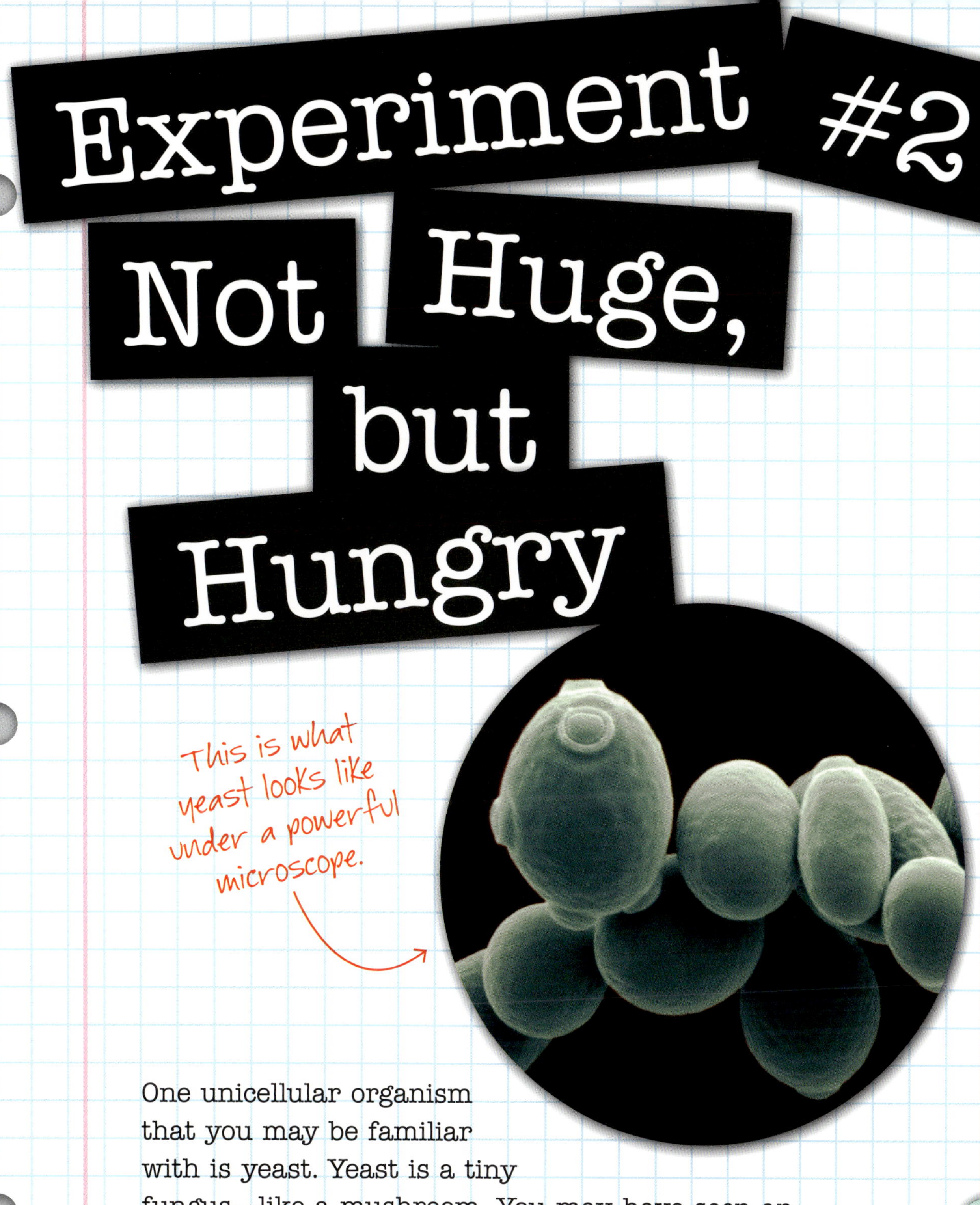

This is what yeast looks like under a powerful microscope.

One unicellular organism that you may be familiar with is yeast. Yeast is a tiny fungus—like a mushroom. You may have seen an adult bake bread with yeast.

Yeast makes bread dough rise.

The grains that make up yeast are very small. If you look at one, you'll observe what seems like a tiny piece of dirt. Don't forget, though, that even the littlest living things are made up of living cells.

A baker mixes yeast with flour, sugar, and other ingredients to form bread dough. The dough is put in a warm place so it can rise. Maybe you've watched this process before. The ball of dough in the bowl gets bigger and bigger over a few hours, until it is overflowing.

What are the yeast cells in the dough doing to make this happen? Study a piece of bread as you search for the answer. Do you notice any holes that look like bubbles or pockets of air? Ask yourself the following question: **Did the changing yeast cells have anything to do with the bubbles or pockets of air forming?** Consider trying out this hypothesis for the next experiment: **Yeast cells cause the bubbles or pockets of air in a piece of bread to form because they produce gas.** Now let's see if you're correct!

Here's what you'll need:

- A packet of baking yeast
- A small bowl
- 1 tablespoon of sugar
- 6 ounces of warm water
- A spoon

You can buy yeast at a grocery store.

Instructions:

1. Empty the yeast into a small bowl, and add the sugar.
2. Next, pour the warm water into the bowl, and stir with a spoon until the sugar is dissolved.
3. Let the mixture stand in the bowl for 20 minutes. Then come back to look at the yeast. What do you notice? Remember to record your observations.

Use warm water, not hot.

Conclusion:

You probably noted that the yeast made gas that took the shape of bubbles. What conclusions can you draw about how the bubbles formed? In bread, living yeast cells consume sugars and produce carbon dioxide gas, which leads to the bubbles that make bread dough rise and create air pockets. Think of sugar as food for the yeast. The yeast cells will be more active if there is more food for them. Now try repeating the experiment, this time using 3 tablespoons of sugar, instead of 1. Does the yeast produce more or less gas?

You have just learned that yeast grains, though tiny, contain living cells. How many living cells make up someone like you? Scientists believe that people are made up of about 100 trillion cells—that's a lot of little parts! Imagine, then, the number of cells that are present in an elephant or the largest mammal on Earth, the blue whale. Blue whales can grow to 100 feet (30.5 meters) long. That's 10 to 17 times more than most adult humans measure from head to toe!

Experiment #3 In and Out—Part One

Can you see the nucleus in each of these cells?

In Experiment #2, you discovered that yeast cells are living things. Even though they are tiny, cells are complicated structures. Different kinds of cells may be built differently, but most share at least a few things in common.

Cells usually contain a nucleus—a structure that acts a bit like the brain of the cell. A jellylike substance called cytoplasm surrounds the nucleus. Certain cell parts are able to travel through this substance. The cytoplasm exists within a cell membrane, a sort of fence that lets things in and out of the cell. Outside the membrane of some cells is the cell wall. Cell walls and membranes serve many purposes, including keeping the different parts of the cell inside.

Look back at your drawings of the onion cells from Experiment #1. Maybe you can label some of the parts now, including the nucleus, the cytoplasm, the cell membrane, and the cell wall.

In order for a cell to work with other cells, the cell membrane must be able to let certain items pass through. Don't forget that cells have to eat. (Do you remember how the yeast cells in Experiment #2 ate the sugar we gave them?) Cell membranes have spaces that allow certain smaller objects in and out.

One of the ways things move in and out of cells is by a process called osmosis. During osmosis, items pass through the cell membrane so that the concentration of certain substances is balanced between the outside of the cell and the inside of the cell. Substances move both in and out of the cell through the membrane to help make this happen.

Keep this in mind as you think about osmosis and water and ask yourself the following question: **How does osmosis affect the water levels inside and outside a cell membrane?** Now consider testing this hypothesis for our next experiment: **During osmosis, the water inside a cell and outside a cell balance each other as closely as possible.** Let's use another onion slice to find out if you're right.

Here's what you'll need:

- 4 tablespoons of table salt
- 1 cup of warm water
- A spoon
- A bowl
- A knife
- An onion

Ready? Let's experiment!

Instructions:

1. Mix the table salt into the warm water, and stir with a spoon until the salt has dissolved. Pour the salty water into a bowl.
2. Use a knife to cut a slice of onion. Ask an adult for help if you need it. Then place the onion slice in the salty water. Let it stand for a few hours. Return to the bowl, and look at the onion. What do you see? Write down all your observations!

Conclusion:

You probably noticed that the onion started to shrivel up or shrink. Why? The water that was in the onion cells passed into the salty water in the bowl. This caused there to be less water present in the onion. Substances pass through a membrane from an area of greater concentration to an area of lesser concentration. Osmosis resulted in more of a balance between the water outside the onion slice and inside the onion slice.

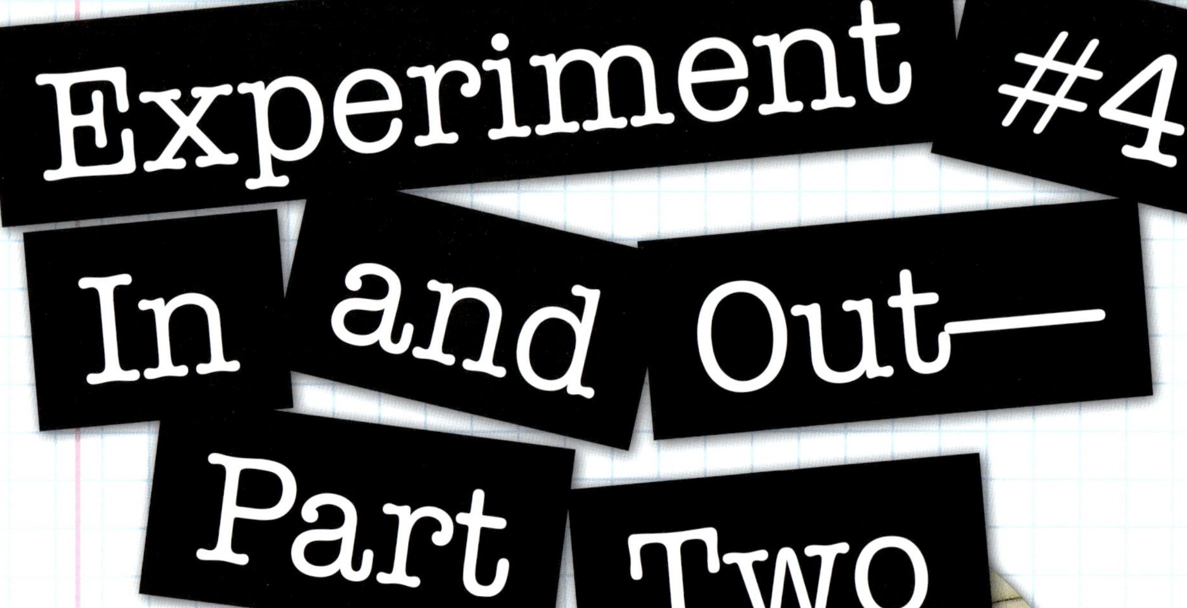

Experiment #4 In and Out—Part Two

Now take your conclusions a step further. Perhaps you've already guessed that if you were to remove the onion from the salty water and soak it in regular water, it would start to expand again. Yet that's something you'd observe with the whole onion slice. You wouldn't see it happen in the individual cells. One question you might be asking yourself is: **Does osmosis cause tiny cells to shrink and expand?** Come up with a hypothesis that will help you figure out an answer. Here are two possibilities:

Onion cells look like tiny boxes stacked on top of one another.

Hypothesis #1: Osmosis *does* cause cells to shrink and expand.

Hypothesis #2: Osmosis *doesn't* cause cells to shrink and expand.

Prepare to discover if your hypothesis is true!

Here's what you'll need:

- A spoon
- 4 tablespoons of table salt
- 2 cups of warm water
- A pair of tweezers
- 2 bowls, labeled Bowl #1 and Bowl #2
- A clean microscope slide
- A clean microscope coverslip
- A water or medicine dropper

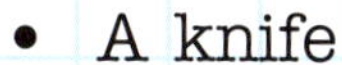

- A knife
- An onion
- A microscope

Your teacher may let you borrow a microscope if you don't have one.

Instructions:

1. Use a spoon to mix the table salt with 1 cup of the warm water in Bowl #1. Then pour 1 cup of plain warm water into Bowl #2.
2. Use a knife to cut the onion in half. Ask an adult for help if you need it. Peel away the 2 outside layers and discard them. With your tweezers, carefully remove a section of the thin skin from the outside of one of the onion halves.
3. Lay the small piece of thin onion skin on the slide, and put the coverslip on top. Gently place the slide under your microscope. Look at the onion cells, adjusting the microscope power and light until you can see them well. What do you notice? Record all your observations, and draw some of the cells you have viewed.

4. Now remove the slide and coverslip. Use your water or medicine dropper to squirt 1 or 2 drops of the salty water from Bowl #1 onto the onion. Set the slide aside for a few minutes. Then cover it once more, and place it back under the microscope so you can look at the onion cells. What do you observe? Draw what you see again.
5. Remove the slide and coverslip one last time, and squirt several drops of plain water from Bowl #2 onto it. Set it aside for a few minutes. Then place it back under the microscope and look at the onion cells. What do you observe now? Keep drawing!

Conclusion:

You probably saw that the onion cells shriveled and shrank in the salt water as fluid left them to make the water outside the cells less salty. Osmosis caused the onion cells to dry out. On the other hand, when you added clean, unsalted water, the fluid flowed into the cell membranes, and the onion cells expanded. In this situation, osmosis restored the cells to what was almost their normal size.

But how can something flow through a cell membrane? Remember that cell membranes are not completely solid. They contain tiny holes. These holes allow certain things to pass through them, but not others.

Experiment #5 Ready to Replace?

Better put on some sunscreen to protect those skin cells!

Cells are amazing structures that never rest. They constantly replace themselves, with new cells taking the place of dead ones. Think of how your skin peels when you get a sunburn. Did you realize that you're

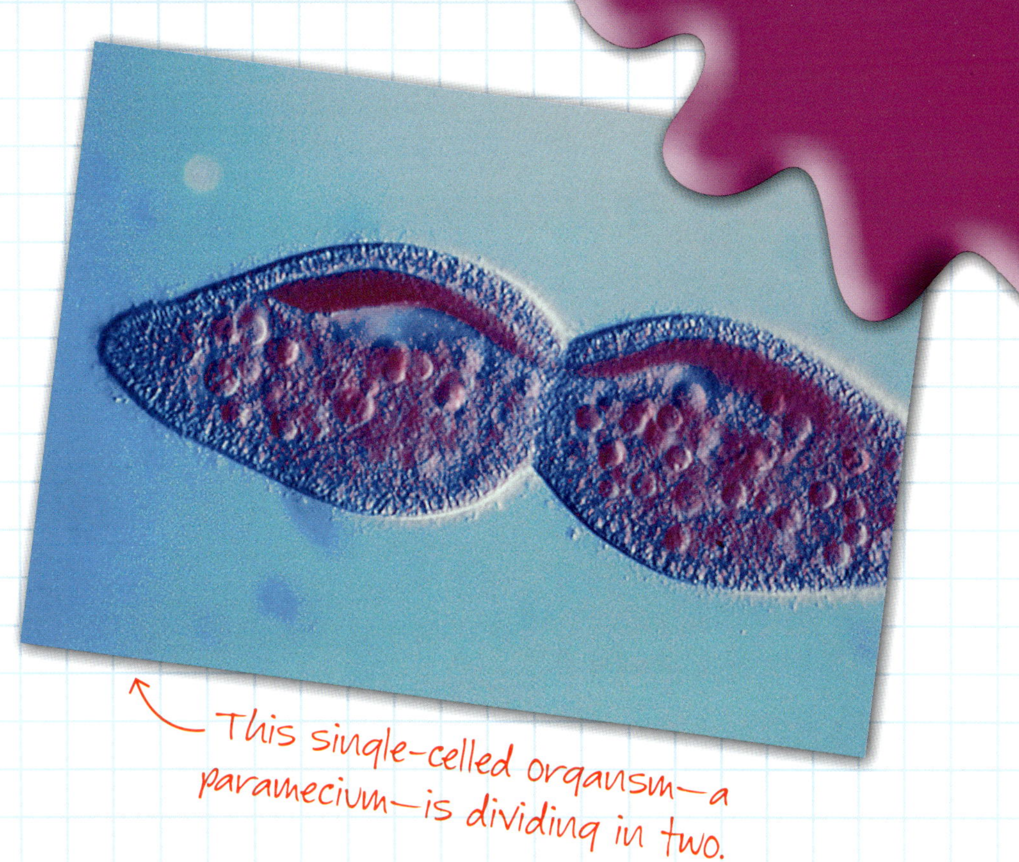

This single-celled organism—a paramecium—is dividing in two.

shedding dead skin cells? And this process doesn't just happen when you forget to put on sunscreen!

See for yourself. Get a piece of colored paper—any dark color will work. Hold your arm over the paper. Now scrub your skin with your other hand. You'll probably see skin flakes fall onto the paper. These are dead cells that you just rubbed off.

When we lose skin cells, other cells work to replace them. A mother cell divides itself into two new cells to replace the dead ones. You observed how your skin cells fell to the paper, but your skin was still okay. You may therefore be asking yourself the following question: **Can other parts of the human body, such as a person's mouth, lose skin cells without suffering lasting damage?** One hypothesis you can test is: **Other parts of the human body, such as a person's mouth, *can* lose skin cells without suffering lasting damage.** Ready to see if you're right?

Here's what you'll need:

- A small spoon or Popsicle stick
- A clean microscope slide
- A water or medicine dropper
- 2 drops of water
- A clean microscope coverslip
- A microscope
- 1 drop of dye called methylene blue stain (Your science teacher may have some, or your parents can help you order some online.)

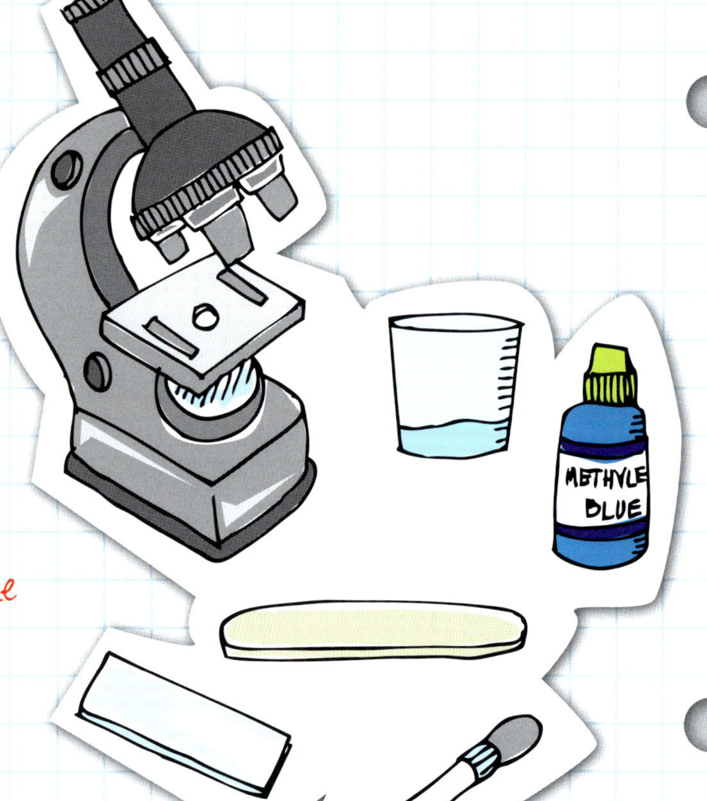

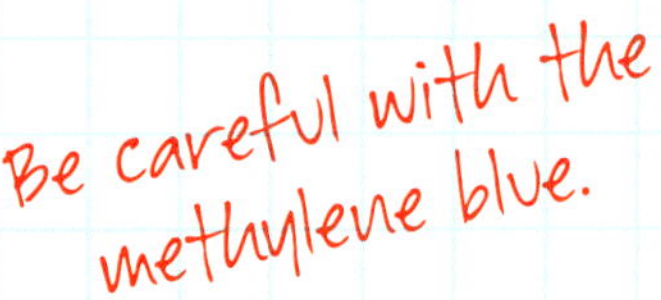

Instructions:

1. Using your tongue, pick a spot to feel on the inside of your cheek. Then ask an adult to take a small spoon or Popsicle stick and gently scrape it against that same area. You want to gather a little material that's nice and gooey! Now feel the spot that was just scraped with your tongue. Does it seem like you're missing anything? Does it feel a little dry?
2. Place a bit of what you collected from your mouth onto your microscope slide. Next, use your water or medicine dropper to add 1 drop of water to the cells you gathered. Then place the coverslip over the slide.
3. Put the slide under the microscope, adjusting the power and light if you have to. Take a look. Do you see cells? Draw what you observe.

4. Now remove the slide and coverslip. Carefully clean both. Repeat the scraping, placing more cells from your mouth onto the slide and adding 1 drop of water. This time, though, add 1 drop of dye next to the drop of water. Gently tilt the slide to mix the color in. Put the coverslip back onto the slide, and look at the cells under the microscope again.

Conclusion:

Can you see the cells better this way? Do you see any of the cells' nuclei? (That's plural for *nucleus.*) Feel the spot in your mouth where you gathered the cell samples. Does it feel different or the same? How do you think your body responded when you removed those cells? Your answers to these questions will help you make your own conclusion.

The human body has many different types of cells—more than 200, in fact. We have skin cells, brain cells, blood cells, muscle cells, and lots of other varieties! Each type of cell does something different. For example, one job of blood cells is to carry oxygen around your body. What other kinds of cells do you think you have in your body? Can you guess what they do?

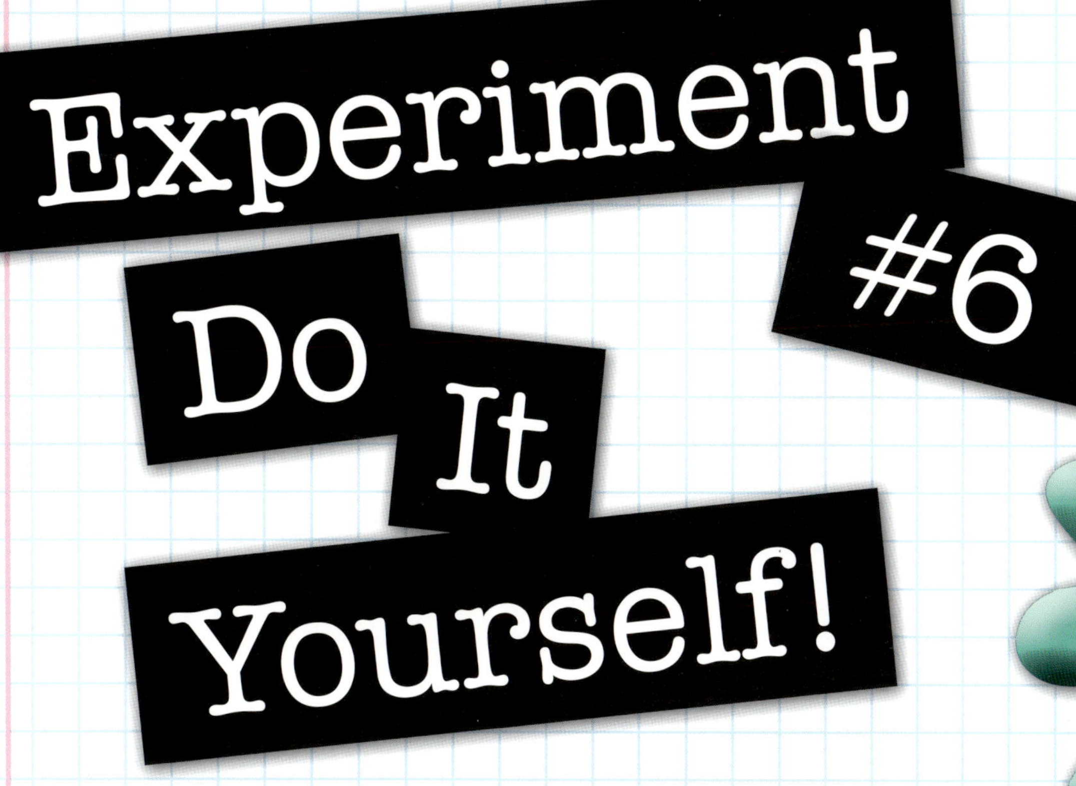

Experiment #6 Do It Yourself!

We have already done several experiments involving cells. But your work as a scientist is only just beginning. How about studying the cell structures of different plants? Or how about comparing your own cells to cells from plants? Why not compare onion cells to cells from the skin on the inside of your cheek? How are the mouth cells different from the onion cells you studied? Do both types of cells have cell walls?

Okay, scientists! Now you've learned about cells through observations and experiments. Do you see how much you can learn and have fun when you think like a scientist?

GLOSSARY

carbon dioxide (KAR-buhn dye-OK-side) a gas that is a compound of carbon and oxygen

cells (SELZ) the smallest living units that make up other living things such as plants and animals

conclusion (kuhn-KLOO-zhuhn) a final decision, thought, or opinion

hypothesis (hy-POTH-uh-sihss) a logical guess about what will happen in an experiment

method (METH-uhd) a way of doing something

multicellular (muhl-tee-SEL-yuh-luhr) made up of more than a single cell

observations (ob-zur-VAY-shuhnz) things that are seen or noticed using our senses

osmosis (ahs-MO-sihss) the process in which a substance passes through a cell membrane until the concentration of the substance on both sides of the membrane is balanced

unicellular (yu-ni-SEL-yuh-luhr) made up of a single cell

FOR MORE INFORMATION

BOOKS

Johnson, Rebecca L., Jack Desrocher (illustrator), and Jennifer E. Fairman (diagram artist). *Mighty Animal Cells.* Minneapolis: Millbrook Press, 2008.

Lee, Kimberly Fekany. *Cells.* Minneapolis: Compass Point Books, 2009.

Stille, Darlene R. *Animal Cells: Smallest Units of Life.* Minneapolis: Compass Point Books, 2006.

WEB SITES

CELLS alive!

www.cellsalive.com

Photos and video clips related to cells

Microscopy4Kids—Cells

www.microscopy4kids.org/webpage/pages/ideascells.html

Video clips of cellular behavior under a microscope

World Carrot Museum—Experiment #4

www.carrotmuseum.co.uk/experiment.html#salt

An easy-to-do experiment related to osmosis and the plant cells that make up carrots

INDEX

About the Author →

Matt Mullins holds a master's degree in the history of science. He mostly writes about science and technology and sometimes about food and wine, culture, and other things that interest him. He lives in Madison, Wisconsin, with his wife and son.